The Weight Loss Scriptures

The 30-Day Daily Devotional for Weight Loss Motivation

Kimberly Taylor

TakeBackYourTemple.com

Please see your health care provider for diagnosis and treatment of any medical concerns, and before implementing any nutrition, exercise or other lifestyle changes.

Table of Contents

Introduction

How great would you feel if you could reach your ideal weight and maintain it for life?

Would you have abundant energy? Look in the mirror and love what you see? Enjoy radiant health?

All of these are good things. In fact, we usually use reasons like these for motivation to lose weight.

The problem is, these motivators do not work on a day-to-day basis.

Think about the last time someone brought hot glazed doughnuts to the office. You tried to remind yourself of the rewards that would be yours if you resisted them. However, you soon started to imagine how good the doughnuts would taste melting in your mouth.

That image eventually won and you didn't have just one doughnut - you had two!

The short-term pleasure overruled the long-term benefit.

But what if you had specific strategies that would help you overcome your daily weight loss challenges?

You would learn how to maintain your focus no matter what.

You would gain confidence that you could pass every test to your resolve.

You would feel good about yourself.

You would have faith that you can reach your ideal weight and maintain it for life.

Sound too good to be true?

It is possible! I was once 240 pounds and a size 22. For over 20 years, I tried many diets and experienced the pain and frustration that often comes with them.

I would start a diet with high hopes, but sooner or later the daily temptations got the best of me. I would revert back to my old habits and I would regain all the weight I lost - and then some.

But one day, I had a chest pain that took my breath away. I was terrified that I was going to die. And in that moment God spoke to me. He said: "It is not supposed to be this way."

I had a choice. Did I believe God or did I continue the cycle I was in?

I chose to believe God. That was the moment my whole life changed.

I ended up losing 85 pounds, going from a size 22 to an 8.

But that wasn't the best part. The best part was that I achieved new intimacy with God during my journey.

I learned to receive His love and to apply His word to my daily circumstances.

I hope to impart these benefits to you on your weight loss journey.

Through the devotions in this book, you will:

- Increase your self esteem

- Gain confidence that you will succeed with your weight loss goals

- Obtain strategies to motivate yourself when are in danger of losing focus

- Find new sources of energy to do all the things you need to do

- Feel at peace with your body and the person God made you to be

All you need is a willing heart in the belief that God is faithful to His word. Are you ready? Then let's get started!

Does God care what you weigh?

A young woman emailed me recently to ask if God cares what you weigh. You too might have seen the title *"The Weight Loss Scriptures"* and think that it means God commands you to lose weight.

Nothing could be further from the truth! God is not in heaven with a scale or a tape measure, agonizing if you gain a pound or two.

He leaves the weight or size you want to be on this Earth up to you, like your hairstyle or shoe choices.

Obviously, it is in your best interest to maintain a size that supports health and energy. Each day, you must decide whether your weight is important enough to you to make choices that impact it for the better.

The bible says that man looks on the outside but God looks on the heart (1 Samuel 16:7).

God loves you just as much at a size 28 as at a size 8.

Nothing you do can make Him love you more than he does now.

What does God care about?

According to 1 Corinthians 6:19-20, our bodies are temples of the Holy Spirit. We are called to glorify God in body and spirit.

In John 15:8, Jesus tells us how we glorify God: "By this My Father is glorified, that you bear much fruit; so you will be My disciples."

The fruit that Jesus is talking about is the fruit of the Spirit. We are to bear **much** love, joy, peace, patience, kindness, goodness, faithfulness, gentleness, and self-control (see Galatians 5:22-23).

Any thoughts or behavior in your life that have become weeds hindering the fruit that you bear concern God.

In my case, compulsive overeating was that behavior – one that I was using to hide myself from emotional pain. My excess weight was just an outward manifestation of what was going on in my heart.

So you see, the real issue is not about size, but stewardship. God can teach you how to become a good steward of your body and remove the hindrances that keep you from bearing fruit.

I recommend you pray the same prayer that King David prayed in Psalm 139: 23-24:

Search me, O God, and know my heart;
Try me, and know my anxieties;
And see if there is any wicked way in me,
And lead me in the way everlasting.

Caring for your body requires wisdom and balance. Only with God's help can you gain both. As I learned to build my health through following Godly wisdom in my eating behavior and through disciplining my body with regular exercise, my weight took care of itself.

Why 'shame and guilt' does not work

I've read many articles about weight loss for Christians, and some seem to endorse the "shame your way to change" approach. But that approach does not work. Well, not for long!

Why? Because shame and guilt ignores the grace of God. Trying to use shame as a motivator ultimately leads to frustration, hopelessness, discouragement, and depression.

But meditating on the grace of God, his goodness, and his love for you constantly leads to a renewed heart and inspires repentance (a change of heart and mind).

You acknowledge that God personally formed every part of your body skillfully and wonderfully, and you want to honor him by taking care of it.

A change in daily behavior is evidence of true repentance.

You cannot disappoint God

The other issue I've seen is Christians thinking they are "disappointing God" by falling short in their weight loss plan. But this too is an error in thinking.

Disappointment comes about when you expect something of a person and are surprised when they don't come through. But God already knows everything about you. He knows about your mistakes before you make them! So how can you ever disappoint him?

Not only that, but he already has a plan in place to help you recover!

Secondly, there is really no way that you can fall short if you use each mistake as a building block, not a stumbling block. What can you learn from the mistake that can propel you forward?

God is ever patient in teaching you the right way and leading you in the way you should go. Remember Philippians 1:6: "...being confident of this very thing, that He who has begun a good work in you will complete it until the day of Jesus Christ".

With that in mind, resolve to never give up on yourself. Hold fast to your confidence.

What is the best scripturally-based weight loss approach?

Scripture says that the kingdom of God is righteousness, peace, and joy in the Holy Spirit. So any thoughts or behaviors that are contrary to God's word, that takes away your joy, and that disrupts your peace concern God.

All of these hinder your ability to fulfill the purpose for which God created you.

Remember that Jesus said that his food was to do the will of God? As his disciples, it is our mission as well.

Let me cover what should be different in how a Christian approaches weight loss. The differences arise from:

- Your identity

- Your reason

- Your method

Your Identity

As disciples of Jesus Christ, our aim is to walk as he walked. In Revelation 1: 5-6, we are told that Jesus through his sacrifice has made us kings and priest to God.

In Romans 5:17, scripture says that we who have received the abundance of grace and the gift of righteousness will reign in life through Jesus.

In contrast, I remember my past struggle with emotional eating issues. I felt out of control with certain foods, feeling they controlled me rather than me reigning over them! And I felt powerless to change the other habits that led to my weight gain.

It was only by assuming my true identity in Christ that I gained victory.

When I had a severe chest pain at 240 pounds and God whispered to me, "It is not supposed to be this way" then I chose to believe him. I had to open myself up to his leading in the way it was supposed to be.

In the process, I admitted my weakness; I asked God for help in prayer daily and walked out the guidance he gave me daily in rooting out the habits that were destroying my health.

I also learned to appreciate my body as the temple of the Holy Spirit. It was not an overnight change, but it certainly is a lasting one!

Your Reason

Jesus said in John 4:34 that, "My food is to do the will of Him who sent Me, and to finish His work." As Christians that is our mandate as well. However, when I was obese and really examined my thoughts, I was shocked to discover how much of them centered around food, not on doing my Father's will.

My main source of joy was thinking about what I was going to eat and when.

But an effective weight loss program teaches us to restore a right relationship to food. God created food for us to enjoy, to give us energy, and to provide the raw materials for our bodies to repair and rebuild themselves.

But food was never meant to control our lives.

Hebrews 12:1 urges all of us, "let us lay aside every weight, and the sin which so easily ensnares us, and let us run with endurance the race that is set before us."

The Method

An ideal weight loss program for Christians would use biblical principles to guide us into reaching our best weight.

When I created *Take Back Your Temple*, one of the guiding scriptures is this one from Proverb 23: 1-3:

"When you sit down to eat with a ruler,

Consider carefully what is before you;

And put a knife to your throat

If you are a man given to appetite.

Do not desire his delicacies,

For they are deceptive food."

Two principles are given regarding eating – eating with wisdom and eating with self control.

Eating with wisdom

You are the ruler in this case since most of the time, you are serving food to yourself. So the guidance is to consider your food carefully. Not be anxious over it, not worry over it, but do consider it.

One thing to consider first is what a privilege it is to have food to eat at all.

As you know, many people in the world do not have food, so it's not a small thing that you have the ability to get food. That's something to be grateful for.

With being able to get food comes responsibility to ensure that the food you eat helps you and doesn't hurt you. Scripture says that some food is deceptive.

Many modern processed foods (those found in a bag, box, or can) impair your body's natural hunger/fullness signals, which can lead to out-of-control cravings and overeating. Remember the potato chip slogan, "Bet you can't eat just one"? It is true! That statement applies to many junk foods and the manufacturers like it that way. The more you eat, the more money for them.

So make it your business to learn about the foods that you tend to eat and the effect they have on your body. I advise you to pay at least as much attention to what you ***put in*** your body as what you put on it.

When you shift your focus from losing weight to building health, your body will naturally reach the weight that is best for you.

Eating with self control

The bible puts it bluntly, *"Put a knife to your throat if you are a man given to appetite."* One of the fruits of the Holy Spirit is the fruit of self control. You already have it but like any muscle, it must be exercised to grow stronger.

One aspect of self control is to learn to eat when your body is hungry. If you have a weight problem, chances are you have disconnected from your body's natural hunger signals.

Proverbs 23:21 says, *"For the drunkard and the glutton will come to poverty, and drowsiness will clothe a man with rags."* The implication here is that when you practice gluttony (overeating), you become drowsy and when you are drowsy, your judgment is impaired.

To hear the voice of the Holy Spirit, your mind must be alert and sharp. But if you are going through life with brain fog (as I was when I overindulged regularly with food) then you are more likely to make decisions that you will regret later.

Discipline your body

I believe that as you increase your physical strength, it enhances your mental and emotional strength. In 1 Corinthians 9:27, the apostle Paul says "But I discipline my body and bring it into subjection, lest, when I have preached to others, I myself should become disqualified."

A regular exercise program shows you vividly that your body is your servant, not your master. Remember that as you go about the work God has called you to, your spirit does not get tired but your mind and body can.

So you want to do everything you can to improve your physical strength, endurance, and flexibility so that your physical condition can better respond to spiritual demands.

Can you eliminate the desire for quick fixes?

I don't believe it is possible to eliminate the **desire** for a quick fix. I think that is part of our sin/flesh nature.

It's like little children on a road trip to Disney World continually asking their parents, "Are we there yet?" When little children want something good, they don't want to wait to get it. They want it now!

But as mature believers, we recognize the truth of the scripture that says that we inherit God's promises through faith and patience (see Hebrews 6:12). Patience is part of the fruit of the spirit and as I mentioned previously with self-control, it must be exercised to grow (see Galatians 5:22).

With that being said, you'll never get to "Disney World" as long as you stay at home. You have to get on the right road to it. Then once you are on the road, you can enjoy the trip by reminding yourself that you will get there in time - encourage yourself continually.

You can also amuse yourself by making your goal a game daily. For example, count how many healthy choices you make each day and every day try to match or beat your previous score.

Finally enjoy the scenery along the way...notice yourself getting stronger, fitter, faster than you were before. Notice better muscle tone. Notice less shortness of breath. All of these will ensure that you will not only enjoy your ideal size when you get it, but enjoy yourself all the way to it.

If weight is an issue for you, you can ask God to show you wisdom in how to handle it.

I am not special - the victory he gave to me, he can give to you! I'll share my secrets in this book.

Weight Loss Scripture Day 1: Choose Life

Today's focus scripture is taken from Deuteronomy 30:19-20

> **"...I have set before you life and death, blessing and cursing; therefore choose life, that both you and your descendants may live; that you may love the LORD your God, that you may obey His voice, and that you may cling to Him, for He is your life and the length of your days"**

I read once that every day, we have to make over 200 choices that impact our health and weight...choices like what to eat, whether to exercise, how to respond to stressful situations, and others.

I didn't believe the number was that high, so for one day, I decided to count the choices I had to make that would impact my health and weight. I counted 78 choices. I was still surprised because I was thinking that it would only be around 30. That is a lot of choices to make in one day!

The scary thing is that most of us make these health choices without thinking about them...influenced by advertising, other people, or just simply repeating the habits of our past.

But there is a bright side. You have between 78-200 opportunities every day that can change your health for the better. Every choice moves you closer to where you want to be. That is...if you choose wisely.

In today's scripture, we are advised to cling to God because He *is* life and the length of your days. Without God, it is impossible to gain the wisdom you need to apply health knowledge to your unique situation. Plus only God knows about the mental strongholds that may be sabotaging your good intentions – and only he gives you the power to take them down!

Today, make a conscious decision to choose life regarding your health. Decide that you are determined to be strong and healthy no matter what.

And then seek God's wisdom in every choice that you make. That way, you can live to the fullest and inspire others to do the same.

Weight Loss Scripture Day 2: Build Your House

Today's focus scripture is taken from Proverbs 14:1

**The wise woman builds her house,
But the foolish pulls it down with her hands.**

Every time I read this scripture, I can't help but think about the story of the three little pigs. In the story, the big, bad wolf was hungry for a pork sandwich and he knew where the three little pigs lived.

He went to the 1st pig's house, which was made of straw, and begged for the pig to let him in. But the little pig would not, so he huffed and puffed and blew the straw house in. But the 1st pig escaped by running to 2nd pig's house.

Then the wolf came to the 2nd pig's house, which was made of sticks. But the 2nd pig wouldn't let the wolf in either. So the wolf huffed and puffed and blew the stick house in. But the two little pigs escaped and ran to the 3rd pig's house.

Then the wolf came to the 3rd pig's house, which was made of bricks. He asked the 3rd pig to let him in but the 3rd pig would not either. So the wolf huffed and puffed and blew with all his might. But the brick house stood.

The wolf blew all day but the house never budged. Finally the hungry wolf went away, determined get an easier meal from other pigs in straw and stick houses!

What about you? Is your house (body) made of straw, sticks, or bricks? Your body is only as strong and healthy as the materials you put into it. Your body turns the food you eat into your bones, blood, skin, liver, and other organs in your body.

Wouldn't you have more confidence in a body built on lean protein, vegetables, and fruits than one built on Twinkies, Ho-Hos, and candy bars?

Now I am not saying that you can't eat such items, but if you want to lose weight and live according to Christian health principles, then I wouldn't advise a regular diet of them.

My goal is to eat healthy 90% of the time or more, saving the other 10% for the other stuff. You get in trouble health-wise when the percentages are reversed!

I think of the unhealthy foods as "tongue ticklers" but I don't attempt to build my body with them as I once did.

With your hands, you have the ability to feed yourself with foods that turn you into a brick house. Remember that old Commodore's song?

Today, be a wise person by building your house with the highest quality building materials, which is eating foods as close as possible to the way God made them.

Weight Loss Scripture Day 3: Keep on Running

Today's focus scripture is taken from 2 Samuel 22:30:

> **For by You I can run against a troop, By my God I can leap over a wall.**

I have a confession to make; when I was a little girl I wanted to be Wonder Woman. I used to watch the T.V. series every Sunday evening, eager to see Lynda Carter as Wonder Woman defeat the bad guys.

My favorite part was always when she would transform from humble Diana Prince to Wonder Woman by removing her glasses and spinning around. A loud noise, fire, and smoke and boom -- her transformation was instant.

Would it be cool if losing weight was like that? All you would have to do is spin around, God would zap you, and all of the weight would disappear. But it doesn't happen that way.

Instead God gives you the endurance to run against troops and leap over walls. That's what King David discovered.

David wrote today's scripture after God delivered him from King Saul, who had been trying to kill him for years. Even though David had defeated Goliath and God had anointed him King over Israel, he still had to fight battles before he could claim what was his.

A strong, healthy body is yours. But you will have to fight for it. Scripture tells us that we do not fight against flesh and blood but against principalities and powers (Ephesians 6:12).

God has strengthened you with the endurance to run against troops, like your habits of the past.

The way you can run with endurance is by giving yourself a vision of what you are running toward, keeping a clear picture of your future healthy self in your mind's eye at all times.

God has given you the ability to leap over walls, like your fears and limiting beliefs.

For example, you might have the fear of failure to leap over. But if you consider failure as a learning opportunity to grow, then you never fail.

Or you might have a fear of success as I once did. Most of my family members are not health conscious.

On some level, I was afraid that if I lost weight and became fit, I would not fit in with them anymore. I would be different and stand out.

But I had to leap over that fear by recognizing that every person is responsible for him or herself. I had to become a good steward of the body God entrusted to me.

The best thing I could do for them is to strive to be a good example and demonstrate that there is a better way to live.

And I could give of my knowledge freely to those family members who asked.

Today, I ask you to recognize that you have extraordinary abilities in God through Christ. Receive them every morning by faith and use them in your daily decisions.

You may not be Wonder Woman (or Superman), but you will get the weight loss results you are after in due season!

Weight Loss Scripture Day 4: Forward Motion

Today's focus scripture is taken from Philippians 3:13:

> **Brethren, I do not count myself to have apprehended; but one thing I do, forgetting those things which are behind and reaching forward to those things which are ahead**

One thing I have learned in my Christian weight loss journey is this: God is a forward thinking and acting God.

I meditated on this fact recently when a scripture from Jeremiah 7:23-24 hit me right between the eyes during my morning bible study time:

> *"But this is what I commanded them, saying, 'Obey My voice, and I will be your God, and you shall be My people. And walk in all the ways that I have commanded you, that it may be well with you.' Yet they did not obey or incline their ear, but followed the counsels and the dictates of their evil hearts, and went backward and not forward."*

Even though God led the Israelites out of Egypt, a place of oppression, wickedness, and idolatry, in their hearts they never left.

Their bodies might have been free in the Promised Land but their hearts and minds were still in bondage back in Egypt.

Too often, we allow fear, emotional pain, and habitual sins to keep us chained to the past. But God sent Jesus to set us free from all that so we can move forward in him.

A wonderful blessing to celebrate!

I heard a motivational speaker once who said that we want the new thing, but still want to hang on to the old stuff! But that just does not work: To experience change, we must change.

When I wanted to be delivered from emotional eating and food addiction, I had a vision: I saw myself huddled in a dark corner, cold, scared, and lonely. And I saw God bathed in light just behind me. I sensed

Him calling me to come to him and give him the emotional burdens that were literally eating me alive. And yet, voices were whispering to me that it was safer in the darkness.

Imagine that: I actually felt safe in my misery!

But God's love was so strong that it compelled me to turn around and look at him in my vision. When I looked, I saw beauty, gentleness, and strength. I trusted Him, took His hand, and haven't been the same.

In order to receive real comfort and move forward, you have to let the false comforts go. Simple as that.

Yes, it takes courage.

Yes, it is scary.

Yes, it is hard.

But say to yourself that you are willing to go to the other side of hard.

That is where your reward is. It is waiting for you. All it takes is a commitment to forward motion, step by step, day by day. And you will get there!

Weight Loss Scripture Day 5: Embrace the Grace

Today's focus scripture is taken from Romans 6:14:

> **For sin shall not have dominion over you, for you are not under law but under grace.**

I receive a lot of emails, and the ones that always sadden me the most are from people who condemn themselves because of their obese state.

And because they condemn themselves and others have condemned them, they think that God must condemn them too.

Nothing could be further from the truth! God is about restoration, not condemnation. He sees differently than human beings see. Think of it like x-ray vision. God can look right past your body, straight into your heart and mind.

He sees all the invisible thoughts and behaviors that contributed to your physical results. And He has the ability to help you change them.

If you have been condemning yourself for your weight gain and generally being unforgiving to yourself then I believe it saddens God. Why? Because through his grace, he has set you free from garbage thinking. Continuing to put yourself down plays straight into the hands of the enemy.

The enemy wants you to be so condemned and discouraged that you get deeper into bondage. But sin no longer has dominion over you. The only power it has is that which you choose to give it.

Remember who your Father is. In your weight loss journey, think restoration not condemnation. Forgive yourself for your past; after all there is nothing you can do about it.

The body you have now is just a snapshot of the choices you made in the past. The choices you make now will determine the body in which you will live in the future.

A necessary part of embracing health is embracing grace. In that way, you can walk in freedom and newness of life, which is the gift that Christ died to give you.

Weight Loss Scripture Day 6: Stay Qualified

Today's focus scripture is taken from 1 Corinthians 9:27:

> **But I discipline my body and bring it into subjection, lest, when I have preached to others, I myself should become disqualified.**

I've made up my mind that I want to be a super-fit 50 year-old. Okay, so I have a few years before I reach that age (God willing), but there is no time like the present to get started.

I think it will be a lot of fun to experience living in a super-fit body at 50 years-old and for a lifetime, so I am going for it!

To go to the next level in my fitness, I joined a 2-week intensive exercise program at one of our local Crossfit gyms. Running, sprints, squats, box jumps, push-ups, pull-ups...military-type exercises.

It was very hard.

The exercises left me sore and sweating buckets!

But I did it because being fit and healthy is important to me. I did it because I want to stay qualified for my life's purpose – which is helping others get and stay healthy.

I really like this statement that the owners of the Crossfit gym wrote about fitness:

> **Fitness is more than just a sculpted physique; it is a state of mind and a way of orienting oneself in the world. To be physically fit in to embody character traits like honor, courage, discipline, integrity, dedication, virtuosity, and joy.**

The exercises in the program were not easy, but I disciplined myself to do them because I wanted the results they brought.

In today's scripture, Paul talks about disciplining his body and bringing it under subjection. When something is under subjection, that means that something else controls it.

In the case of your body, your mind is supposed to control what it does. But too often, we fail to exercise that authority!

A vivid example of that was played out in the media not too long ago.

A well-known athlete cheated on his wife with multiple women. Even though he disciplined his mind to excel in his sport, he failed to discipline his mind to resist temptation.

And because of this, his body led him into a situation that hurt his wife, damaged his family, and caused him to lose respect from those who admired him.

As Paul said, when you fail to bring your body into subjection, it can make you disqualified. Continuing the previous example, the athlete was disqualified from some current and future revenue opportunities because of his actions.

When it comes to your weight loss goals, you too must be careful to be a person of integrity, which means wholeness. You keep your word to yourself and others. And your actions match your words.

I've seen many examples of people who say that being healthy and getting fit is important to them, yet they act in ways that will bring them the exact opposite result. It seriously damages your confidence and esteem when you say one thing and do another.

So today, resolve to go to the other side of hard by disciplining your body. It starts with disciplining your mind. You can control your thinking and direct your thoughts where you want your body to go.

As I said in the *Take Back Your Temple* ebook, the mental work you do to get fit and healthy is much harder than any physical work you will do.

But if you keep your eyes on the prize, you will win and stay qualified for the purpose to which God has called you!

Weight Loss Scripture Day 7: Escape Temptation

Today's focus scripture is taken from 1 Corinthians 10:13

> **No temptation has overtaken you except such as is common to man; but God is faithful, who will not allow you to be tempted beyond what you are able, but with the temptation will also make the way of escape, that you may be able to bear it.**

Every one of us has areas in which we are vulnerable to temptation and the devil knows exactly what they are. Imagine this scenario:

You are at your desk at work. You get hungry and are tempted to get a bag of cookies from the vending machine. You have an apple in your desk that could ease your hunger better, but a voice whispers "You know you don't want that." So the movie begins.

You see yourself eating the cookies. You think about how the cookies will taste and how the sugar buzz will feel after you eat them. Without even being aware of it, all of the memories and associated feelings of eating cookies come upon you.

You suddenly find yourself digging in your purse for change so that you can get those cookies. What happened? You've just been seduced by Temptation T.V.

Channel 666 on your mental dial, Temptation T.V. is designed to put you in bondage. It broadcasts 24 hours a day, seven days a week and its programming caters to your weaknesses.

For example, if chocolate fudge cake tempts you, then Channel 666 will show you video of the most decadent, gooey chocolate fudge cake you can find.

Channel 666's goal is to drag you down to the gutter. To do this, it must create desire within you so it makes its images appear even better than the real thing. But it never lives up to its advertising.

Whenever you find yourself being tempted, check to see if your mind is tuned into Channel 666. What pictures are running through your head? If the pictures are those of the object that you are attempting to resist, then you are tuned into Temptation T.V.

When you find you are tuned into Temptation T.V., just look up. That's right, look up at the sky or the ceiling or whatever happens to be above your head. Just the simple act of looking up reminds you to focus on God. It also interrupts the pattern that you have established for tuning in to Temptation T.V. That pause allows you to change the Channel to 777, Truth T.V.

What does Channel 777 focus on? It focuses on those things that support your desire to implement God's will in your life: those things that are true, noble, just, pure, lovely, of good report, anything worth of praise (see Philippians 4:8). So if you find yourself on Channel 666, then look up and tune into Channel 777.

Next, think or say in faith, "Lord, I am being tempted. Your word says that I am able to bear this temptation and I believe your word. Show me the way out of this temptation right now and give me the strength to choose that path. I receive the escape and the strength right now in Jesus' name."

Whatever the Holy Spirit tells you to do, then do it immediately. The more you tune in to Channel 777, the weaker the signals get from Channel 666.

And here is one more thing to do to escape temptation. Do not keep foods in your house that tempt you. I had a woman write me years ago about her weakness for cookie binges.

She had some in her cabinet and said that she was being tempted to eat them. She said that she didn't know why the Lord didn't just remove the temptation from her.

Well, I am sure the Lord told her that she needed to get rid of the cookies and that was the way he provided for her escape. But the truth was (and I have been there) that she wanted it both ways.

She wanted to keep the cookies close so that she could still eat them. She was making provision for her binges!

I've written many times about the fact that I love the taste of Pepperidge Farm coconut cake and how I used to buy a cake with the intention of just eating one slice a day. But it never happened. I would always eat up eating the whole cake in one sitting.

I had to face the fact that this food is a weakness of mine. Even though it has been years since I ate a whole cake, I don't tempt myself by bringing cake into my house. I no longer make provision for binges.

See, I believe that the best way to win a fight is to avoid getting into one in the first place. So when it comes to temptation, the first step to escaping is to make sure that your food temptations are removed from your living spaces – at home and work.

But if you must face them, then turn to Channel 777 and look for the escape route. God has prepare the path for you, all you have to do is take it!

Weight Loss Scripture Day 8: In Due Season

Today's focus scripture is taken from Galatians 6:9:

> **And let us not grow weary while doing good, for in due season we shall reap if we do not lose heart.**

The most common question I get via email regarding weight loss issues is this: "I've been eating healthy for (*fill in number*) weeks, but I've only lost (*2 or 3*) pounds. What is going on?

First of all, it is easy to lose heart if the scale is your only measurement of progress. After all, weighing yourself is the worst possible measurement of fat loss. And fat loss is what you want, right? Losing water or muscle weight will hurt you in the long run and that is what happens on the so-called "quick weight loss" diets.

Scale weight is a combination of the weight of your bones, muscles, organs, body water, skin, other elements, and fat. What you are really after is a change in body composition – shapely muscles and less fat.

A better indication of progress regarding your body composition is how your clothes fit. Has your clothing size decreased in that time period? If you are taking measurements (a better indication of changes in body shape), are they smaller than they were?

See, 5 pounds of fat takes up much more room than 5 pounds of muscle.

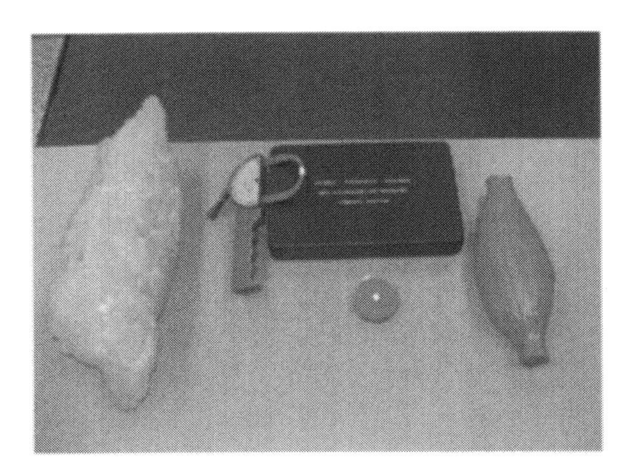

The 5 pounds of fat is on the left and the 5 pounds of muscle is on the right. Now notice how the fat is lumpy, jiggly, and shapeless.

In contrast, the muscle is smooth, compact, and shapely. Muscles are the hardworking laborers of your body. Skeletal muscles move your body around.

Fat, on the other hand, is along for the ride. I always think of fat cells as freeloaders!

Actually, they would help you survive in a famine but I don't recall a widespread famine happening in America recently.

Now let's say that you lost 5 pounds of fat, but gained 3 pounds of muscle. The scale would only say that you lost 2 pounds. But you got rid of fat the size of the image on the left. That is a lot of fat!

The next time you go to the grocery store, pick up a pound of Crisco or butter to see how heavy even 1 pound of fat is. That's less "freeloader" weight you have to carry around.

In addition, you should see how your body composition changed for the better, which would show up in the smaller clothes size or body measurement.

In the *Take Back Your Temple* small groups, participants are strongly encouraged to take measurements rather than weigh. We also encourage them to also pay attention to other signs of improvement such as:

Boosted energy	**Increased confidence**
Improved quality of sleep	**Greater mental focus**
Enhanced shape and muscle tone	**Increased muscle strength**
Improved flexibility	**Better mood control**
Added glow to your skin	**Enhanced balance and coordination**
Improved endurance	**Increased sexual enjoyment**
Reduced depression	**Increased ability to handle stress**
Improved circulation	**Clearer skin**
Freer breathing	**Increased optimism about life**
Improved joint discomfort	**Amplified desire to tackle other life goals**

All of these are signs that you are moving in the right direction! However, if you only use the scale, then you give it power to discourage you and make you want to quit.

And quitting increases your odds to 100% that you won't get the body and level of health you want.

If you stay on track, all the while using the previously mentioned signs as milestones that you are moving in the right direction, then you can have confidence that you will reach your new size in due season.

Now, about due season. That is another thing that irks me about quick weight loss diets – they prey on the impatient. Jesus often used farming principles to teach spiritual principles.

With the principle of sowing and reaping, there is a time to plant, a time to cultivate, and a time to sow. You don't just plant one day and harvest the next.

And yet quick weight loss diets and get rich quick schemes would have you believe otherwise.

Whenever I read a diet that touts that you can lose "30 pounds in 30 days" my automatic question is "30 pounds of what?" It is easy to manipulate the scale with water losses or gains. But that does nothing for improving your body shape or building your health.

If you lost it fast, you'll gain it back faster! I speak from experience because I fell for those schemes for over 20 years. It was only when I focused on building my health and allowed my faith and patience to work together that I received permanent results.

I hope the above tips will help you "have heart" while working on your goals. Renew your mind with today's scripture if you find yourself losing heart and in due season, you will reap if you don't give up.

Weight Loss Scripture Day 9: Get to Work

Today's focus scripture is taken from Proverbs 21:25:

> **The desire of the lazy man kills him, For his hands refuse to labor.**

When I first read the above scripture many years ago, it really convicted me.

For many years, I would **say** that I wanted to get healthier and lose weight, but my efforts were half-hearted at best. And when the slightest opposition appeared and things got too hard, my good intentions would collapse like a house of cards!

However, there is nothing like having excruciating chest pain to fuel your desire to get healthy! Unfortunately, that is what it took for me to make my health a top priority.

And I am so grateful to God that he gave me a 2nd chance because I know all too well that, instead of a warning, the chest pain could have been the beginnings of a fatal heart attack.

You are the only one who can decide if losing weight and getting healthy is important enough to put daily time and effort into it. Some people make a conscious decision that good health is not worth it and are willing to live with the consequences of that decision.

But the bible gives a devastating example of the results of neglect in Proverbs 24:30-34:

I went by the field of the lazy man,
And by the vineyard of the man devoid of understanding;
And there it was, all overgrown with thorns;
Its surface was covered with nettles;
Its stone wall was broken down.
When I saw it, I considered it well;
I looked on it and received instruction:
A little sleep, a little slumber,
A little folding of the hands to rest;
So shall your poverty come like a prowler,
And your need like an armed man.

If you decide that reaching and maintaining a healthy weight is an important goal for you, then do yourself a favor for your health's sake and work on it every day no matter how long it takes - until you get the result you want.

In today's focus scripture, the bible gives two clear choices when you desire something - you either work for it, or you give up that desire.

It makes sense because it is misery to want something but refuse to do anything about it - if you are in a position to do so. I call it "killing knowledge."

It is killing knowledge because deep inside, you know that you are capable of so much more. Your confidence and self-esteem drop lower every day that you hang on to that desire without working for it.

You feel life passing you by and the only thing you have to look forward to is a future of regrets. It's a sad, sad way to live!

But if you do something to get closer to your goal every day, no matter how small it is, at least you will have the satisfaction of knowing that you are working on making your dreams come true. You are no longer ignoring them but through your actions, you tell yourself, "Yes, I am worth it."

Because you are! Now roll up your sleeves and go to work!

Weight Loss Scripture Day 10: Number your Days

Today's focus scripture is taken from Psalm 90:12:

So teach us to number our days,
That we may gain a heart of wisdom.

How many times have you said to yourself, "Where did the day go?"

Sometimes when you think about how you spent your time, you can't remember half of what you did.

Here is one of the greatest lessons I have learned in my weight loss journey: *I would never gain control over my life unless I gained control over my day.*

The bible asks you to live mindfully each day. When you acknowledge how limited your time on earth is, as the scripture advises, you understand how important it is to use that time wisely.

Taking care of your health is certainly a wise use of your time. The late motivational speaker Jim Rohn once said, "Some people don't do well because they don't feel well."

Having a healthier body will enable you to enjoy your life more and have greater energy to make an impact on others.

Since you want to lose weight then a certain part of each day must be spent on making sure that you stay on track with your health goals.

Just to give you some ideas, here are a few things that I do to stay on track with my goals:

- I keep a fruit bowl stocked on my dining room table, usually with apples, pears, oranges, and occasionally bananas, to make it easy for me to have a healthy snack when I get hungry.

- I take time to fill up a water jug so that I can drink water regularly throughout the day.

- I take time to batch cook on Saturdays and put meals in the freezer to make it easy to eat healthy when I get busy during the week.

- I take time to schedule what exercise I plan to do each week and post it on the refrigerator

- I take time to mentally review the vision I have of the level of fitness I want to achieve. I remind myself that every day, I am moving closer to my goal

- I take time to pay attention to any discouraging thoughts that are contrary to God's word and I take them captive to the obedience of Christ as the bible instructs us to do (2 Corinthians 10:5).

So decide what your priorities are and resolve to set up your daily life to spend time on them.

And at the end of your life, you will have the satisfaction of knowing that you spent your time on this earth wisely and that you made a difference!

Weight Loss Scripture Day 11: Eliminate Food Triggers

Today's focus scripture is taken from 1 Corinthians 6:12:

> **All things are lawful for me, but all things are not helpful. All things are lawful for me, but I will not be brought under the power of any.**

Boy did food once have power over me! Back when I was 240 pounds, if you asked me if I wanted some chocolate chip cookies, warm from the oven, my eyes would gleam, my heart would race, and my mouth would water. I'd practically be rubbing my hands with glee.

In hindsight, it is the anticipation a drug addict would probably have who was about to get a fix. And it wasn't just chocolate chip cookies that caused that reaction...it was any food that had sugar in it. One big discovery I made in my weight loss efforts is that I am extremely sugar sensitive.

Sugar is my trigger food. When I eat or drink a lot of it, it makes me not only want more sugar, but also want to eat more of everything else!

Whether the sugar comes from fruit juice, soda, white flour products, or dessert, it causes a specific physical response within me if I eat or drink too much of it.

It's like being tipsy from alcohol – mellow, brain fogged, slightly out of it. I also feel lazy, like I don't want to do anything but sit, lie down, or nap. This makes sense when you know that alcohol itself is nothing but fermented sugar!

I spent most of my adult life living in that state, cycling between sugar hits and crashes. Everything seemed fine as long as I was in the sugar haze. But when the sugar wore off, life was too real, vivid, painful, and overwhelming.

Sugar at first was my treat, but then it became my crutch to get through life.

I couldn't even imagine my life without sugar in it.

When a substance has such a hold on you that you can't even imagine life without it, then it has power over you. It hurt me to admit that sugar had power over me but as long as I refused to admit it, I continued to give it power to wreck havoc on my brain chemistry and my body in the excess weight gain.

So I had to put aside my pride and admit the truth and seek God's help to stop "pulling the trigger" and destroying my health with sugar.

If you have a weight problem that is behavior based, then you have food triggers too. Just think about which foods that you eat regularly and which ones cause you to break out in a cold sweat at the thought of never having them again. That is your food trigger. That is the one that has power over you.

The bible says that you are not to be brought under the power of any *thing*. Food is a *thing*. So you will need Godly wisdom and empowerment to get free, which is yours for the asking.

You may get wisdom on how to eliminate the trigger or make a substitution that doesn't cause such a strong physical reaction within you. For example, I can tolerate high-fiber fruits just fine because the fiber within the fruits slows the release of sugar, so I don't have the loopy feelings. But if I drink a large glass of fruit juice (which has no fiber), then I get loopy and ravenously hungry after the sugar wears off.

I always advise keeping a food journal for a while and write down how certain foods make you feel so that you can begin to shift your diet to those foods that make you feel and do your best. It will make it easier to succeed with your Christian weight loss efforts in the long run too!

Weight Loss Scripture Day 12: Be Transformed

Today's focus scripture is taken from Romans 12:2:

> **And do not be conformed to this world, but be transformed by the renewing of your mind, that you may prove what is that good and acceptable and perfect will of God.**

Many of you know today's scripture, but have you taken time to meditate on it or better yet, to use its prescription to reach your Christian weight loss goals and transform your life for the better?

With the *Take Back Your Temple* ebook, I spend a lot of time at the beginning discussing how to renew your mind because after so many years of diet failures, I finally decided to do things God's way and it was the only thing that worked for me.

So I wanted to save you some time and show you what works. And just as I am showing you in these daily scriptures, I took God's word and meditated on it. I made an effort to apply that word to my daily life and I can say by personal experience – God's word works!

Think about it: in Hebrews 11:3, scripture says that the world was framed by the words of God. We live in the world so wouldn't it be in our best interest to frame our lives according to that word so that our lives work the way God intended?

In the scripture, it says that when our mind is transformed, we prove what is that good and acceptable and perfect will of God.

Concerning our health, God has made it perfectly clear that he wants his people healthy. In Jeremiah 33:6, he says that he will bring health and healing to the land and reveal to his people the abundance of peace and truth.

Now for each of us, health means different things. For some, just being without disease is an acceptable level of health. For others, it means to be energetic and able to do daily activities easily. Still others, it means to be fit, strong, and at their ideal weight. And finally for others, it means to be an athlete, fit enough to play sports with ease.

Each of us gets to define at which level of health we would like to live, but make no mistake about it...God's will is for us to be healthy!

If you look around in this world right now, you see an abundance of lethargy, sickness, stress, and deception. But that is because the world does not know God or his word. For us Christians, we are called to live differently because God's presence and his word is near to us. All we have to do is seek him.

I'd recommend regularly reading scriptures that give you a picture of God's view on health and healing, and then implement wellness principles in your life that will support the level of health at which you want to live.

As for me, my big dream is to be fit enough to score excellent for the Navy Physical Readiness test for my age group. That means I would have to be athlete fit and I'm not there yet (they have the guidelines posted on the Internet).

Why the Navy PRT? Well, before I started nursing school, I seriously considered joining the Navy because I was interested in the Navy Nurse Corps. With my nursing degree, I could have entered the Navy as an officer, plus they had great benefits.

I even had a Navy recruiter come to my house! But as soon as he started talking about having to shoot firearms, I knew that wasn't the career for me!

Still, I've always admired the fitness level the military requires of its personnel and I wondered what it would feel like to be so fit that you can conquer any physical challenge.

So I have upped my fitness game to get to that level. Not only that, I am also having to become more mentally tough to get past the discomfort of the training.

But I have made up my mind that it will be worth the effort. I'd like to have that experience in my lifetime.

So what's your health dream? Renew your mind to support that effort. Define it, think it, speak it, and live it, knowing that God supports you all the way. And you will be transformed!

Weight Loss Scripture Day 13: See Good Days

Today's focus scripture is taken from 1 Peter 3:10:

For "He who would love life
And see good days,
Let him refrain his tongue from evil,
And his lips from speaking deceit.

I would guess that the primary reason you want to lose weight is that you want to love life more and see more good days. Sure you can say that it's just about looking good, but doesn't looking good make you feel good too?

Or if you want to lose weight so that you can perform better, doesn't that make you feel good too?

The bible provides a good prescription on how you can love life and see good days now – before you even lose a pound! The prescription will also help you with your Christian weight loss goals.

See, when I was a teenager, I used to call myself "fat". In hindsight I wasn't even overweight, but after high school, I became so. And soon, I graduated to obese. It was a self-fulfilling prophecy!

Be sure that the words you speak to yourself are ones you want to answer to. It is important to recognize that you may have excess fat on your body but it is not who you are. Saying that you "are" fat is as ridiculous as saying "I am blood" or "I am bone". Just as they are parts of you, your fat is part of you...for now until you shed the excess that you don't want.

So when you say "I am" think about this: "I AM" is the name of our Father. Therefore, "I am" are the two most powerful words in the universe. What you say after those words is very important. While your "am" is lowercase, it still has power.

Speak kindly to yourself and about yourself. If you are anything like me, it will feel strange at first to give yourself encouragement, compliments, approval, and validation – things I was seeking so desperately from other people.

I came to recognize that I was speaking evil to myself, constantly comparing myself to other people and finding myself wanting. Every day I was hurting myself with my thoughts and words, and all I was doing by consuming the cakes and pies was trying to soothe the hurt that I was inflicting on myself!

So once I saw the pattern and started befriending myself, then I had less need to emotionally overeat. Does that make sense?

The less I overate, the more my body started shedding the excess fat. And the more excess fat I lost, the better my performance and the better I looked. I started loving life and seeing good days!

Examine how you speak about yourself, even going as far as to imagine that the words you are saying to yourself as ones that you are saying to a little child who longs to have your love and approval.

Would you *still* say those words to them?

If not, then don't speak that evil to yourself either! Encourage yourself and speak well of yourself. And more good days will be yours right now.

Weight Loss Scripture Day 14: Perfect Peace

Today's focus scripture is taken from Isaiah 26:3:

> **You will keep him in perfect peace, Whose mind is stayed on You, Because he trusts in You.**

This is one of the most practical prescriptions for health in the bible and yet one of the toughest ones for us to follow!

This scripture came to me as I found myself worrying about a particular situation. The more I thought about it, the more anxious I became.

Then I thought, "Wait a minute. Jesus said that his yoke is easy and his burden is light (Matthew 11:30). I am feeling burdened right now. Something is wrong!"

Instantly, today's scripture popped into my head and I closed my eyes and started meditating on God's goodness. I meditated on situations that I had once thought were impossible to overcome, yet God brought me through.

A wonderful feeling of peace and calmness came over me after a while, proving the truth of the scripture.

So it will be for you too. The more you meditate on your problems, the more anxious you feel. The more you meditate on your solution (God), the more peace you feel.

This reminds me of some research I did because I was curious as to why Jesus referred to his followers as "sheep". And I found out some interesting facts about them from Wikipedia that says a lot about how we are expected to behave:

Sheep:

- * In general, sheep have a tendency to move out of the dark and into well-lit areas

- Sheep prefer to move uphill when disturbed

- Sheep have a tendency to congregate close to other members of a flock

- In displaying flocking, sheep have a strong lead-follow tendency

So as sheep, when we are disturbed, our first instinct should be to move "uphill" and seek the light of God's presence and his word. We also should seek other believers who can help support us during times of vulnerability.

Finally, we should strive to hear God's voice so that we can follow where he would have us go.

In contrast, Jesus called those who were not his "goats". Here are some interesting facts about goats:

Goats:

- Goats are reputed to be willing to eat almost anything, except tin cans, and cardboard boxes

- Goats will test fences, either intentionally or simply because they are handy to climb on

- Being very intelligent, once a weakness in the fence has been discovered, it will be exploited repeatedly

- Goats readily revert to the wild if given the opportunity

Goats resist any and all boundaries, continually wanting to have their own way. Even though the Shepherd set up the boundaries to protect them, somehow in their minds they think they know better and seek to climb over the boundaries just because they can.

Goats, in spite of their intelligence, do not act from wisdom but from self-will. They are well known for their combative nature, while sheep are known for being peaceable and gentle. Which would you like to be?

I've had "goat days" but thankfully they are rare now. I have learned the wisdom of keeping my mind stayed on the Shepherd who knows the past, present, and future. A Shepherd who loves me and has my best interest at heart.

My Shepherd promises that all things work together for my good because I am called according to his purpose (Romans 8:28).

If you find yourself being anxious about any aspect of your Christian weight loss plan or anything else in your life, then re-direct your mind to your Shepherd and receive the peace that surpasses all understanding!

Weight Loss Scripture Day 15: Anchor your Soul

Today's focus scripture is taken from Psalm 5:3:

My voice You shall hear in the morning, O LORD;
In the morning I will direct it to You,
And I will look up.

One of the most important principles I teach with the Take Back Your Temple process is to anchor yourself in God.

However, I also know that it is the step, along with renewing the mind, that many people skip with their Christian weight loss efforts.

This is a mistake.

See, with all the stress and temptations in the world, you need to be anchored to deal with these negative forces in a healthy way.

Without anchoring, you will be pulled in multiple directions and end up doing only what is easy and convenient, whether it is in your long-term best interest or not.

Without anchoring, the world dictates to you what to do rather than you teaching it what to do - guided by your Father's wise counsel.

As Deuteronomy 4:7 says, *"For what great nation is there that has God so near to it, as the LORD our God is to us, for whatever reason we may call upon Him?"*

In today's scripture, the Psalmist says that in the morning, he directs his voice toward the Lord and that he looks up. I can't think of a better way to start your morning than to talk to your Father in prayer - and listening for his voice as he talks to you.

Even if you can only manage 10 minutes to start, it will set the tone for your entire day.

By setting this time aside, you are communicating to God and yourself that you are putting him first in all things.

Starting your morning in prayer is a wise thing to do because the Father knows what challenges you are going to face that day. And through prayer, he can give you the strength you need to face them.

He will also give you the ability to glorify him (demonstrate his character) in everything you say and do.

Remember in the Lord's prayer (Matthew 6:9-13) how Jesus asked the Father to lead us not into temptation but deliver us from evil? That is definitely a request to make in your daily prayer time because you do not want to have to fight any unnecessary battles with others or yourself.

When you seek the Lord in the morning, your spirit is refreshed and you find yourself being more optimistic and faith filled.

You also gain a higher view of life when you look up. You recognize that getting healthy is not just about you, but having the ability to make a more positive impact on the people around you.

You face life with your head held high, with courage, determined to do what it takes to reach your goal, glorifying God in body and spirit!

Weight Loss Scripture Day 16: Renew your Youth

Today's focus scripture is taken from Psalm 103:2-5:

> **Bless the LORD, O my soul,**
> **And forget not all His benefits:**
> **Who forgives all your iniquities,**
> **Who heals all your diseases,**
> **Who redeems your life from destruction,**
> **Who crowns you with lovingkindness and tender mercies,**
> **Who satisfies your mouth with good things,**
> **So that your youth is renewed like the eagle's.**

Yippee! I mentioned in a previous message, I participated in a two-week intensive exercise workshop called Crossfit. It was intense, but I finally graduated. I feel really good that I was able to finish it.

I thought I was in decent shape but this pushed me in ways I never imagined.

Our instructor said that the experience should change what fitness means to us and he was right. It convinced me even more that since I only have one life to live, I want to live it fit!

I know this will be especially crucial as I get older, God willing. When I was home health nursing, I saw clear examples of aging gracefully vs. aging poorly.

One lady in particular stands out for me. Her doctor ordered a few home nursing visits after her surgery. So I was assigned to check her vital signs and wound to ensure that no signs of infection existed.

This lady was in her 70s at the time, yet she looked 20 years younger. She was moving freely around her home with an energy that was astonishing, especially given that she had had surgery just a couple of days before.

When I commented on how great she looked, she told me that during the time of World War II, she was taught to eat one red vegetable, one orange vegetable, and one green vegetable every day. She had done this without fail.

She also said that back then, she started a habit of exercising daily too, which she did consistently.

She was living proof that good, daily health habits add up – and they pay off. I wish I could say that most of the patients I saw were like her, but they weren't.

Most were barely able to get out of bed. They were full of physical complaints and the slightest physical activity left them breathless. They had to take expensive medications just to keep the symptoms of their sickness at bay.

In today's scripture, one of the benefits listed that God provides is that he satisfies your mouth with good things so that your youth is renewed like the eagles.

I believe that he provides two things that satisfy your mouth – good words via the bible and good food, which is the food he placed on this earth specifically for the human body to eat to function at its best.

I believe the more you fill your mouth with these good things, the more your youth will be renewed!

I can testify to this. Just a few years ago, I saw a woman who hadn't seen me in 15 years. Back then, I was still obese. But when she saw me recently she said, "You look younger now than you did then!"

Mind you, I was in my late 20s then so it was quite a complement.

I certainly feel better now than I did then. I am able to do a lot of things that I wasn't able to do then. I can run, jump, skip, and play.

I even challenged one of my teen-aged cousins to a foot race – and won! It feels great to be fit.

As part of your Christian weight loss goals, don't just consider the difference healthy habits will make in your immediate future. If God should grant you long life, how do you want to live it as you age? Do you want to be strong, healthy, and vibrant? Or do you want to be weak, sick, and sad?

Your choices now determine which future you will be living in. So choose wisely!

Weight Loss Scripture Day 17: Clothed in Strength

Today's focus scripture is taken from Proverbs 31: 25-27:

Strength and honor are her clothing;
She shall rejoice in time to come.
She opens her mouth with wisdom,
And on her tongue is the law of kindness.
She watches over the ways of her household,
And does not eat the bread of idleness.

Many of us have read Proverbs 31. It describes a woman who is strong, honorable, kind, industrious, diligent, takes good care of herself and her household.

Most of all, it describes a woman who reverences the Lord and puts him first in her life. She lives in perfect balance.

Regarding Christian health, there are many tips we can take away from the Proverbs 31 woman. First, it says that she was clothed in strength and honor – so much a part of her that other people could see it.

But her strength was not natural strength – rather it was strength derived from her personal relationship with God.

The scripture also said that she rejoices in time to come. In Psalm 21:1, the psalmist identifies that the source of joy is our recognition of God's strength.

Because the Lord is strong and mighty, we become strong and mighty as we abide in him, able to overcome any obstacle he calls us to overcome.

Continuing the scripture in Proverbs, it says that the Proverbs 31 woman opens her mouth with wisdom and speaks with kindness. With this prescription, there is no room for "shooting from the lip".

We all know people who speak without thinking, who speak whatever comes into their minds, no matter who it hurts.

But God calls us to speak with wisdom and to speak kindly. We are to speak the truth but in love, both to others and ourselves. Most of all, we speak

God's word to edify ourselves and others because God's word brings health to our flesh (Proverbs 4:20-22).

Lastly, the proverbs says that the Proverbs 31 woman watches over the ways of her household and does not eat the bread of idleness.

This woman uses her God-given influence to benefit her family. As she works on her own health, she uses her influence to improve the health of her family as well, one healthy choice at a time.

She keeps her home neat, clean, and organized because she knows that a peaceful environment facilitates health as well. With her home organized, she can spend more time on those things that matter most.

But even if this woman's house was in disarray, then she would strengthen herself to get it back under control, one corner or section at a time if necessary.

The Proverbs 31 woman recognizes that being physically active is not just good for her body, but for her mind and emotions as well. She takes time to rest but does not allow rest to descend into laziness by neglecting the important tasks in life.

It takes strength to do the right thing, but by following the example of the Proverbs 31 woman, you can put on the strength God provides to you daily and operate your life in a way that brings glory and honor to him!

Weight Loss Scripture Day 18: Get the Right Support

Today's focus scripture is taken from Ecclesiastes 4: 12:

Though one may be overpowered by another, two can withstand him. And a threefold cord is not quickly broken.

I can't overemphasize how much easier you can make your Christian weight loss efforts by having an accountability partner. I think that was another reason for my success in losing my 85 pounds. But I had to pick the right person.

When I was seeking to change, I discovered that the friends in the same shape as I was could not help me.

All too often, if they suggested not exercising that day or going to eat at a place where our favorite tempting foods were served, I was only too happy to say "just this one time" and agree to it.

Before I knew it, we had all abandoned our health goals, only to complain again months later about how unhappy we were about being out of shape.

This cycle continued for years.

However, after I had my chest pain, I was super-motivated to conquer this issue in my life once and for all. I wrote down tactics that seemed to work for me in the past and what didn't.

Then I got an idea: Suppose I asked someone in great shape to be my accountability partner?

And I knew just the person. A co-worker of mine was in excellent shape. She ate healthy and worked out consistently. We were the same age but she looked 10 years younger than me simply because she had taken care of herself over the years.

It wasn't easy, but I put aside my pride and asked her to help keep me accountable. I kept an eating and exercise checklist each week that I created myself and every Monday, I showed her what I did the previous week.

I talked about what I thought I did well and what I wanted to work on that week.

She didn't coach me, but just having someone to share victories and struggles with was a great motivator. Knowing that Sandy was going to see my food log on Monday was often enough to make me think twice about overeating!

She even invited me as a guest to her gym a couple of times and I saw for myself what dedication to staying in shape looked like.

I saw how she took time to prepare healthy lunches to bring to work. I knew that if I wanted those same results then I too had to change how I managed my life so that I made time for being healthy.

Regarding today's scripture, you already have God on your side since he never leaves you or forsakes you. I've already discussed how important it is to ask for his help through prayer in previously.

But it also helps to have human support and accountability.

If you do have a friend who is in the same shape that you want to use as an accountability partner, be careful; ask about her reasons for wanting to get in shape...does she intend to make it a lifestyle to be fit or do she just want to shed pounds temporarily for the class reunion?

You need someone to support you who has made up her mind that she wants to be healthy long term.

In addition, does your friend operate with integrity in other matters? If she tells you that she is going to do something, does she usually follow through?

If you have learned through experience that you can't count on your friend's word, then that is another clue that she would not be a good accountability partner for you.

But as I said, the best accountability partner is one who has already successfully achieved what you want.

And if you don't have access to the one person, then small group support is a great option as well. The bible says that in a multitude of counselors, there is safety.

So think about ways you can get support for your goals. That way, if you find yourself getting weary in doing good, you've got someone who can back you up and help you keep moving forward!

Weight Loss Scripture Day 19: Build that Wall

Today's focus scripture is taken from Proverbs 25:28:

Whoever has no rule over his own spirit

Is like a city broken down, without walls.

In the book of Nehemiah, the people of Israel purposed to re-build the wall around Jerusalem, which its enemies had destroyed. In ancient times, cities were frequently overrun, its possessions plundered and its people carried off to be slaves. So having a wall around the city was a necessary means of protection against such an event.

Many years ago, God revealed to me that taking care of our health is like building a wall of defense for our bodies. What have you done today to build that wall?

Unfortunately, many people are tearing down their walls, brick by brick with the choices they make. This is evident by the growing statistics of obesity and all the diseases that go with it like diabetes, heart disease, stroke and others.

In Proverbs, it says that if you don't rule your spirit, you are like a city broken down, without walls.

What is your spirit? It is your mind, your will, and your emotions.

Whenever you do not submit your thoughts, will, and emotions to the obedience of Christ, you leave yourself vulnerable to temptations and addictions.

Alcoholism, Gluttony, Drug Addiction, and all others are just symptoms of the chaos occurring in people's spirits. And eventually, this chaos is physically manifested on their bodies.

But with God's help, you can be set free; peace and order can be restored and a wall of defense built.

In the *Take Back Your Temple* ebook, a key step in the process is to 'Expect Tests and Be Prepared'. Part of building a wall of defense is to set up your environment to minimize temptations and to make it easier to go the way you want to go. You consider what foods and situations have sabotaged you in the past and you make plans for handling them.

Use your past experiences as building blocks for your wall of defense rather than stumbling blocks to keep yourself stuck.

If you find yourself habitually experiencing negative emotions like depression, anger, and others first take them to the Lord in prayer and then seek out healthy ways to deal with them in the natural.

Decide today that your health will be a priority and that you will build that wall of good health. You will feel stronger, more emotionally stable, and more secure – all qualities that will help you get maximum enjoyment from your life.

Weight Loss Scripture Day 20: Handle the Little Things

Today's focus scripture is taken from Luke 16:10:

> **He who is faithful in what is least is faithful also in much; and he who is unjust in what is least is unjust also in much**.

There is an old song lyric which says that "Little things mean a lot." That is true in so many things in life, especially when it comes to your Christian weight loss goals.

Back when I was 240 pounds, I had a habit of ignoring little things.

Procrastination was my best friend!

I would let bills pile up, then when I would look at them, I'd discover they were past due so I had to pay expensive late fees on top of what I already owed.

I also ignored the state of my house. I let clothes pile up until they overflowed my clothes basket. It was only when I had to step over the clothes to get to the basket that I would deal with them.

I let dishes pile up in the sink until the kitchen looked like a tornado had gone through it. Only when the mess was so severe that I couldn't ignore it anymore did I deal with it.

I had clutter everywhere – desk piled high with paper so that I had to dig through it to find important documents. Only when I became so frustrated that I couldn't deal with the pile any longer did I deal with it.

As I mentioned previously, this chaotic way of living was only a reflection of the emotional chaos inside of me.

Most telling of all was how I ignored myself. The only "self care" I allowed myself was to eat. And soon, this "little thing" became a big issue in the excess weight it caused me to gain.

Only when I had a severe chest pain and thought I was going to die did I make up my mind that I was going to deal with the excess weight permanently.

Do you see a pattern here?

When God woke me up to what was going on inside of me, and began to heal my emotional pain, he showed me how important taking care of little things are.

He showed me how even taking small steps to improve my life makes a big difference over time – as long as I took them every day. Consistency is the key.

So today, now that I have lost the 85 pounds and have reached the perfect weight for me, I really strive to take care of the little things in my life.

I pay my bills on time so that I don't give those businesses more money than necessary.

I wash the dishes so that they don't pile up in the sink.

I wash clothes regularly, fold and iron them either the day of washing or the day after so they don't pile up.

I won't say doing these things is always pleasant, but taking care of them when they are small is a lot easier than having to deal with them when they become a big pile! Reminding myself of that fact is often enough to spur me to action.

And I no longer ignore myself either. I take time for stretching, hot baths, candles, soothing music, hobbies, exercise, and other forms of self care. I still like to eat, but it no longer has the significance in my life that it once did.

I make sure that most of what I eat not only tastes good, but builds my health too.

My life is so much easier now and I have **much** less stress.

Think about how you are living – is your life in order? Are you handling the little things before they grow into a big mess?

In the focus scripture of the day, Jesus had just taught the parable of the unjust steward. This steward had not managed his master's resources well and had to give an account of his stewardship to him.

Everything that we have belongs to God, including our bodies. Someday, we will have to give account to him on how we used the resources he gave us, whether we used them wisely or unwisely.

God watches how we use our earthly resources to determine whether to entrust us with more. So if you want bigger rewards in life, then start handling the little things you deal with on a daily basis faithfully – in all areas.

Weight Loss Scripture Day 21: Guard your Mouth

Today's focus scripture is taken from Psalm 141: 3-4:

Set a guard, O LORD, over my mouth;
Keep watch over the door of my lips.
Do not incline my heart to any evil thing,
To practice wicked works
With men who work iniquity;
And do not let me eat of their delicacies.

When I first read this scripture, I chuckled because I thought that this could be a dieter's prayer! Not "dieter" in terms of deprivation, but one who wants to be discerning about what passes through the doors of her lips.

I am not sure whether David was speaking about being discerning concerning the things entering his mouth through the foods he ate or about things exiting his mouth through the words he said. The scripture could apply to both, but I'm inclined to think he was speaking more about the things exiting his mouth.

In Matthew 15:11, Jesus said to the Pharisees who were offended because his disciples did not wash their hands before they ate bread, "Not what goes into the mouth defiles a man; but what comes out of the mouth, this defiles a man."

Jesus was saying that what you eat does not make you dirty or unclean spiritually, but that which comes out of your mouth. What you speak reveals what is going on in your heart. As the scripture says, *"Out of the abundance of the heart, the mouth speaks"* (Matthew 12:34).

While being discerning about the words you speak is priority, I believe you must set a guard regarding the foods you eat as well.

Now it is true that the foods you eat do not make you spiritually dirty or unclean, but they do affect you physically.

For example, if there are certain foods that you eat that sap you of energy, then you have to decide if you need to guard against them entering your mouth.

If you fail to set a guard, then you are choosing to allow them to rob you of energy, which leads to living a low energy life.

I wrote about the importance of handling little things previously and this is certainly a case of little things (food choices) having a big impact over time.

So if you are having trouble with un-beneficial foods entering your mouth or un-beneficial words exiting your mouth, then know that through today's scripture you can ask God for empowerment to handle both!

Weight Loss Day 22: Limit the Sugar

Today's focus scripture is taken from Proverbs 25:27:

> ***It is* not good to eat much honey;**
> **So to seek one's own glory *is not* glory.**

I've written about sugar addiction a lot simply because it was the biggest physical factor in my weight gain.

After many years of writing down what I eat and paying attention to how certain foods make me feel, I have keen knowledge now of what foods benefit my whole body and which don't.

I have to admit that I love the taste of sweet things. And in fact, I am not alone because scientists say that we are genetically inclined to prefer the taste of sweet foods.

That was one way our ancestors could tell the difference between foods they could eat freely and poisonous foods (usually bitter) that would kill them!

But a critical shift has happened in our food supply over the last fifty years and obesity has exploded (pardon the pun) over the last decades. The primary cause is our new reliance on foods in bags, boxes, and cans.

Most of these man-altered foods have a secret ingredient added to them: yes, you guessed it - sugar!

If you eat a lot of processed foods, fast foods, and junk foods, you are probably eating more sugar than you realize. And if you drink a lot of fruit juice and eat a lot of white flour products (bread, pastas, and others), then these break down quickly into sugar as well.

I don't believe that sugar the way that God made it is bad in small amounts - after all, God described the Promised Land as a land of milk and honey!

However, I do believe it is not good to eat a diet heavy in sugars as man has altered them. The body simply does not recognize them as real food.

For example, high fructose corn syrup is a recent concoction in which man has boosted the fructose content of regular corn syrup, itself a processed food. Fructose is fine when it is contained within a fiber matrix the way God designed it in whole fruit, but take it out of that environment and the body processes it as a poison.

For more information about that, I recommend you watch a video on YouTube entitled "Sugar – the Bitter Truth."

In addition, white sugar is bleached to make it white when it is refined from sugar cane. Again man has taken sugar cane, a food that God made and turned it into another product entirely that plays havoc with the body's natural hormonal balance.

High sugar intake interferes with Leptin, which a natural hormone that tells you when you have had enough to eat. A high fructose diet has been shown to contribute to overeating and obesity.

I have observed that when I eat a lot of sugar, not only does it make me crave more sugar, but it makes me want to eat more of everything else. So it is not a case of will-power; my body has a very specific reaction to sugar almost like an allergy.

That is the way I view it now. I may take a few bites of something sweet, but more than that and I start feeling brain fogged and hungrier.

I recognize the feeling very well, and because I don't want to live that way anymore, then I avoid the foods that trigger it.

I recommend you visit the following website and see if you recognize the signs of sugar sensitivity in yourself: radiantrecovery.com.

So be wise – recognize the foods that your body doesn't like. By that I mean **your whole body**. Even if your tongue likes it, but the rest of your body doesn't, then consider your tongue outvoted!

Don't allow your tongue to become the little dictator that is controlling and ruining your life. Instead make it your friend in that you seek foods that taste good, but also benefits every organ and cell in your body!

That means making foods the way God made them the cornerstone of your diet. That means fruit, vegetables, lean proteins, complex carbohydrates, and healthy fats. And you can enjoy honey – but as the bible advises, don't eat much of it.

Weight Loss Scripture Day 23: Inherit the Promises

Today's focus scripture is taken from Hebrews 6: 11-12:

> **And we desire that each one of you show the same diligence to the full assurance of hope until the end, that you do not become sluggish, but imitate those who through faith and patience inherit the promises.**

This scripture gives you awesome wisdom on what is needed to obtain the promises of God: faith and patience. You need both to sustain yourself long enough for the promise to come into your life. Otherwise, you will abort it.

A couple of weeks ago, I heard a pastor define faith as expecting the best from God. I think you can only expect the best from God when you know his character and when you know his word.

In one of my favorite scriptures, the bible says of God's character (Numbers 23:19):

"God *is* not a man, that He should lie,
Nor a son of man, that He should repent.
Has He said, and will He not do?
Or has He spoken, and will He not make it good?

With this in mind, then you can expect the best from God when he says:

For I will restore health to you

And heal you of your wounds,' says the LORD (Jeremiah 30:17)

To strengthen your faith, you must create and keep a picture in your mind of what health looks like to you. I actually recommend writing that vision down and reviewing it regularly.

I had a woman write me once to say that she had read my website and material, yet still wasn't healed from her food addiction.

The Holy Spirit led me to ask her if she could see her life without the food addiction as part of it.

She never responded back to me.

I suspected that she could not even picture her life without it.

And if she couldn't see herself putting away the addiction, then she would never be free of it.

There is a reason why God told Abraham that he would number his descendants as greater than the stars of heaven and the sand as the seashore.

He gave Abraham a visualization to hold on to of the promise, one that would encourage and comfort him during the waiting.

Because Abraham knew that God would not lie to him, when he pictured the number of his descendants as the stars and sand, then his heart would be filled with joy because he knew that it was good as done.

And the joy of the Lord is strength!

The second requirement to inheriting God's promises is patience, which is simply the ability to wait and watch as we take the appropriate actions needed to obtain the promise - day by day.

It sounds so easy, but we all know that it is not!

When God promises us something good, we want it right now! Remember my example of the little children on a road trip to Disney World asking their parents constantly, "Are we there yet?"

But as they mature, the children learn to trust their parents.

Even though sometimes they might get tired of waiting during the drive or get bored with the scenery, they don't start doubting that their parents are taking them to Disney World.

To pass the time, they might imagine what they are going to do once they get to Disney World (a sign of faith that they believe they will get there) or they might encourage themselves by watching for milestones that they are headed in the right direction.

Regarding your Christian weight loss goals, be just as diligent and determined that you will inherit the promises that God has for you. With faith and patience working in you, they are yours!

Weight Loss Scripture Day 24: Consider your Meditation

Today's focus scripture is taken from Philippians 4:8:

> **Finally, brethren, whatever things are true, whatever things are noble, whatever things are just, whatever things are pure, whatever things are lovely, whatever things are of good report, if there is any virtue and if there is anything praiseworthy—meditate on these things.**

Have you ever thought about what you think about most of the time? When I had a weight problem, I can tell you what I thought about most of the time: food!

I once saw a program called "I eat 33,000 Calories a Day" that featured severely obese people and one quote a lady said in that program stuck with me.

She said, "Food is the first thing I think about in the morning; it's the last thing I think about before I go to bed."

There was a time when I could identify with that statement, but not anymore. Because God has taken his rightful place in my thoughts – first – then food no longer controls my thinking like it once did.

The bible says that we should first seek to think about those things that are true. As Christians, our final authority for what is true is the word of God.

So if we are thinking something that is contrary to the word then we are called to renew our minds by replacing that thought with what is true.

For example, if you are thinking about retaliating against a person who has hurt you, then you recall and meditate on what the word of God says about the situation: *"But I say to you, **love your enemies**, bless those who curse you, do good to those who hate you, and pray for those who spitefully use you and persecute you"* (Matthew 5:44).

Or if you are thinking giving in to a habitual temptation then you replace that thought with wisdom from God which says, "**No temptation** has overtaken you except such as is common to man; but God is faithful, who will **no**t allow you to be tempted beyond what you are able, but with the **temptation** will also make the way of escape, that you may be able to bear it." (1 Corinthians 10:13)

How about if you are feeling led to give up a certain food that causes negative effects in your body, but you are thinking that you can't live without it?

You can meditate on a scripture such as Romans 14:17 which says, "for the kingdom of God is not eating and drinking, but righteousness and peace and joy in the Holy Spirit."

I challenge you today to consider the thoughts you have most often on a daily basis. Are they true, noble, just, lovely, of good report, or praiseworthy? If not, then seek God's wisdom to help you renew your mind to those thoughts that glorify him.

I guarantee that you will experience more inner peace, which will be evident in your outward circumstances!

Weight Loss Scripture Day 25: A Confident Witness

Today's focus scripture is taken from Isaiah 43:10:

"You are My witnesses," says the LORD,
"And My servant whom I have chosen,
That you may know and believe Me,
And understand that I am He.
Before Me there was no God formed,

Nor shall there be after Me.

In today's focus scripture, God gave the Israelites two identities. He said that they were his witnesses and they were his chosen servants. As Christians today, we are also called to be witnesses but instead of servants, we are now called God's sons and daughters through our faith in Jesus Christ (Galatians 4:6).

But I want to focus on what it means to be a witness because knowing this can help you greatly during tough times, including those related to your Christian weight loss goals.

As God's witness, that means that you are qualified to testify of him to others about your personal experience with him. This is not "book learning".

It means that you have had an up close encounter with him and you have seen his power demonstrated in your own life.

Nobody can argue with that because it is your personal testimony.

But how can you be a witness to something that you haven't seen?

Think about being a witness in a courtroom trial. If you try to testify of what somebody else said, what somebody else saw, or your own theories then that is not admissible evidence. That court will call it *hearsay*.

You know this if you've ever watched *Judge Judy*!

The court will only admit as evidence that what you personally observed, heard, or experienced.

To make you his witness, God has to make the pages of the bible come alive for you.

As he guides you through the trials you face, you come to know his character of love, faithfulness, and longsuffering.

You come to know him personally as Savior, provider, and healer.

So it is through involving God in your daily life that you come to know and delight in him. You come to rely on him to help you through life.

You can't imagine living any other way and as a result, when you speak to others about God and his son Jesus, the truth and authenticity of your witness will be very persuasive.

See your weight loss goals as an opportunity to involve God in the smallest details of your life. And when you lose weight and people ask how you did it, you can tell them about God's faithfulness in helping you get there.

Nobody seeks out hardships in life, but if they do come then invite God in and watch him work. He will show himself strong on your behalf and you can't help but witness to others about what he has done for you!

Weight Loss Scripture Day 26: Walk in the Spirit

Today's focus scripture is taken from Galatians 5:16:

> **I say then: Walk in the Spirit, and you shall not fulfill the lust of the flesh.**

Today's scripture gives you the ultimate secret of overcoming any bad habit or addiction – walking in the Spirit. But I want to explain how something as simple as the foods you eat can interfere with walking in the Spirit.

The apostle Paul defines one of the lusts of the flesh as idolatry (Galatians 5:19-21). Did you know that food obsession is a form of idolatry?

In Philippians 3:19, Paul spoke of people whose god was their belly. That described me once. I thought it was just an issue of self control, but I was wrong.

I loved God but I did not realize that the way I was eating left me vulnerable to food obsession and thus, to food idolatry.

And I believe millions of people are in the same boat.

Many people like myself are sugar sensitive. When they eat it, it causes a specific reaction in their bodies similar to a drug. It can be sweets, crackers, or other white flour products – any food that raises the blood sugar quickly.

It is part of their chemical make-up, the same as anyone who suffers from allergies.

Because the effect is drug-like, over time they require more and more sugar/white flour products to get the same effect. Eventually, they become so hooked on the pleasure the substance gives them, that their thoughts become preoccupied with it.

Thus, a stronghold is set up in their minds and food idolatry is born.

If you are in this cycle, the first thing you need to do is take the issue to God in prayer, asking him to reveal to you those foods you are habitually eating that you are "allergic" to.

That's how I have to think about this issue in my own life because by thinking of it as an allergy, that lets me know how serious it is.

Ask God to show you natural foods that you can add to your diet that will help re-balance your body. Most of these will be in the fruit and vegetable category, wholesome foods that God made specifically for our bodies.

Next spend regular time in prayer, praise, worship, and study of God's word.

As you replace thoughts of food with thoughts of God, you will tear down that mental stronghold.

The obsessive thoughts must be replaced; you can't just tell yourself not to think about food. That's about as effective as telling yourself not to think about a pink elephant! Try it now and see what pops into your head!

As you replace thoughts of food with thoughts of God, you will become stronger and able to make wiser choices daily. And as you make wise choices and operate in self control, then you will reach your Christian weight loss goals faster than ever before!

Weight Loss Scripture Day 27: Celebrate Small Victories

Today's focus scripture is taken from 2 Corinthians 2:14:

> **Now thanks be to God who always leads us in triumph in Christ, and through us diffuses the fragrance of His knowledge in every place.**

I love this scripture because it is assurance that no matter what challenges we face, as long as God is leading us, we are destined to win!

It is critical to recognize when working on your Christian weight loss goals that you are working from a position of victory as long as you don't quit.

So many people wait until they reach their goal to celebrate. However, it is important to write down and recognize the small victories you have along the way. This is a great encouragement.

Did you eat a serving of vegetables whereas you weren't eating any before? That is a victory.

Drank 4 glasses of water today when you drank 3 yesterday? That is a victory.

Took a walk around the block today when you weren't doing any exercise previously? That is a victory too!

In fact, in my *Take Back Your Temple Healthy Habits Journal*, which the small group program uses, I have a section for each day's entry called "What I Did Well Today". It is a place for you to acknowledge your small victories.

Too often we focus on the mistakes we make and completely ignore the things we are doing right. And that is not right.

When you acknowledge what you are doing right, that gives you confidence and the good feelings you get will make you want to accumulate more small victories. And those small victories add up to big results!

Here is one more reason to celebrate small victories today – tomorrow is not promised to you. Sure, I believe in setting goals for the future, but I also recognize that whether I live to see that future is up to God. So I make the most of each day, enjoying the body that I have today while enjoying the steps I am taking to change it for the better.

Now if I do in fact get to the future to enjoy my results, then so much the better. But in the meantime, I focus on doing my best every day – celebrating the process.

If you do the same, you will not only enjoy the weight loss process more but you will appreciate your results more when you get them!

Weight Loss Scripture Day 28: What do you Expect?

Today's focus scripture is taken from Isaiah 41:10:

> **Fear not, for I am with you; Be not dismayed, for I am your God. I will strengthen you, Yes, I will help you, I will uphold you with My righteous right hand.'**

I am always filled with confidence when I read the above scripture, especially the knowledge that God is upholding me. But today, I want to talk about the first part of the scripture, in which God says to "Fear not".

Fear is the number one reason that people do not obtain all God wants them to have.

I heard an awesome way to look at fear just the other day. Dax Moy, a personal trainer in the U.K., defined fear in this way: "**F**orever **E**xpecting **A**wful **R**esults".

Consider the scenario in Numbers 13, in which God charged the Israelites to go into the Promised Land. Out of the 12 men appointed to spy out the land, 10 of them brought back a bad report.

They said they couldn't conquer the land because the giants in it were stronger than them.

They were expecting awful results to come about if they did what God told them to do.

However, Joshua and Caleb thought differently. They remembered that they had God on their side. And so they expected to be able to conquer the land.

In Numbers 14, God commended Caleb for having a "different spirit" in him. He and Joshua were the only two men from the original spies to ultimately live to see the Promised Land.

Check what you are expecting today in your weight loss goals. Are you expecting the best (faith) or are you expecting awful results (fear)?

What you are expecting determines which mindset you are living in.

And only the mindset of faith will get you the best results!

Weight Loss Scripture Day 29: Rejoice!

Today's focus scripture is taken from Ecclesiastes 5:19:

> **As for every man to whom God has given riches and wealth, and given him power to eat of it, to receive his heritage and rejoice in his labor—this is the gift of God.**

The word for today is to enjoy yourself! One of the fruits of the spirit is joy and one of the best reasons to rejoice is that you have been redeemed from sin and given new life in Jesus Christ.

God has given to every one of his children the gift of riches and wealth. This is not always financial abundance, but it does mean possessing things of great value. Good health is incredible wealth.

I agree with the late author Issak Walton who said: "Look to your health; and if you have it, praise God, and value it next to a good conscience; for health is the second blessing that we mortals are capable of; a blessing that money cannot buy."

And of course, the first blessing is that God claims us as his own!

Whatever steps you are taking to reach your ideal weight or improve your health, rejoice in them. Yes, it may be hard, but so what? If you have decided that you are going to do it, then why make it harder for yourself by complaining about it?

Better to re-direct that energy into getting the job done.

Praise God for giving you the wisdom to recognize the value of good health and to take steps to protect yours.

Seek out things today that you are grateful for. Be more present-minded – as the old saying goes, "Yesterday is history, tomorrow is a mystery, so rejoice in today – that is why they call it 'the present.'"

Today, start opening up your present and rejoice in the steps you are taking to change your health and life for the better!

Weight Loss Scripture Day 30: God's Nutrition Prescription

Today's focus scripture is taken from Genesis 1:29:

> **And God said, "See, I have given you every herb that yields seed which is on the face of all the earth, and every tree whose fruit yields seed; to you it shall be for food.**

I hope you have enjoyed reading this scripture series as much as I have enjoyed writing it! For the last scripture, I am led to start at the beginning with one of God's first instructions to man – telling him what he was to eat!

This scripture came to me from a lecture I attended given by Dr. Joel Fuhrman, the author of the books *Eat to Live* and *Eat for Health*.

In his talk, Dr. Fuhrman gave some startling facts: By age 45, 99% of Americans have atherosclerosis – which means that fatty plaques have collected on the walls of their arteries, causing poor circulation.

It is at the root of heart disease, strokes and other diseases.

But he said that the nutrients in green vegetables over time cause these fatty plaques to become more "slippery" and eventually they slide off and the body breaks them down clearing the artery.

As the doctor was saying "Science has shown..." I could not help but think about Ezekiel 47:12 in which the prophet said, "Their fruit will be for food and their leaves for medicine."

Science is just confirming what God already said in his word over 2,000 years ago!

It makes sense that these fruits and vegetables should be the baseline of our diets since we are merely following the recommended fuel that our bodies' designer said was best!

But the problem according to him is that most Americans are addicted to the processed, man-made foods. Because these foods provide no nutrition, the average person is literally starving for nutrients even though they may be obese.

I know that was true of me; When I weighed 240 pounds, I lived off fast, junk, and processed foods. I would feel good immediately after eating them, but then came the crash—I would feel drugged, lethargic, sleepy, irritable, anxious, and depressed. To feel good again, I was compelled to overeat the same kinds of foods.

It so sad that so many people live in and accept poor health. They think it is normal to live the first part of their lives with low energy, irritability and emotional upsets.

They think it is normal to live the last half in gradual physical decline, their bodies breaking down, sick, in pain, mentally confused, and finally dying in a hospital hooked up to machines.

It is not supposed to be this way. We can be mentally sharp, strong, and vital practically all the way up to death.

God's will is that we stay healthy. And the best prescription for that is the nutrition prescription in Genesis 1:29. I recommend taking it as seriously as you would a prescription from your doctor.

Dr. Fuhrman's recommendation was to eat 2 cups of green vegetables every day and eat 1 large green salad every day (go light on the dressing and ensure that it doesn't contain High Fructose Corn syrup). He also recommended eating 3 fruits a day.

While this is not all you can eat, at least work your way up to making these your baseline foods, ensuring that you always get your "medicine" inside you daily, if nothing else.

Now, I know a lot of people who don't want to eat healthy. They would like a loophole in which they can have a baseline diet of processed foods and still be strong, energetic, clear minded, and healthy.

But think about this: Suppose one day you decide that you don't like the smell of gasoline and from now on, you are going to fill your car tank with rubbing alcohol. You decide that you like the smell of rubbing alcohol better.

So you do it.

Here's the 45 million dollar question: Do your actions change the fact that gasoline is the fuel your car was designed to run on?

No.

Is it likely that your car will be damaged by not using the right fuel?

Absolutely.

Why take those chances with your body and health? It's true that you you might be that 1% of Americans that don't have atherosclerosis by age 45. But the odds are stacked **way** against you.

You can view Dr. Fuhrman's list of healthiest foods on his website *eatrightamerica.com*.

You don't have to eat only from the top foods but at least it helps to make better decisions about what to eat.

I hope this information helps and that you live healthy and well!

Bonus Encouragement for your Weight Loss Journey

I hope that you have been blessed by this book. Each day, you must continually remind yourself of these principles.

Otherwise, it's a case of "Out of Sight, out of mind."

So be diligent to renew your mind.

Also be careful that the names you call yourself are ones you want to answer to.

I once received an email from a man who called himself "fatty" and "coward". Here was my message to him and I hope you take it to heart:

Brother, you are insulting the one whom God has created! Before you can even change your outside, your mind must be renewed to the truth of what God says about you.

Nowhere in the bible do I see God condemning a person for being overweight – and certainly God did not call anyone "fatty!" In fact, there are only two instances in the bible that I know about in which a person was described as a fat person.

One of them, Eli, was God's priest.

God did not rebuke him for being heavy – he rebuked him for allowing his sons to dishonor God in their temple service.

See, God always deals with us at the heart level – regardless of what we look like on the outside.

The religious people of Jesus' day looked good but their hearts were far from God. Jesus described them as "white-washed tombs full of dead men's bones" (Matthew 23:27).

For many years I put myself down like you are doing. I started when I was 12 – calling myself fat even though in hindsight I wasn't. Now I know how powerful words are.

Eventually "fat" became my mental identity and then it became my physical reality.

I had to learn to love myself at the size I was – before I even lost a pound. I had to renew my mind to what God says about me first.

God commands us to love our neighbors ***as*** *ourselves. That word "as" is important – to me, it means that God expects us to love ourselves.*

Furthermore, it means that our love of others will be limited if we cannot even love ourselves!

Here's what I want you to do the next time you find yourself calling yourself "fatty" or "coward". Memorize these scriptures and use them to combat those lies. Jesus resisted the devil's temptations with God's word and that is how you will win the battle in your mind as well:

> ***Psalm 139:14***
> *"I will praise You, for I am fearfully and*

wonderfully made; Marvelous are Your works, And that my soul knows very well."

2 Samuel 22:33-35
"God is my strength and power,
And He makes my way perfect.

He makes my feet like the feet of deer,
And sets me on my high places.

He teaches my hands to make war,
So that my arms can bend a bow of bronze."

My prayer for you is this: That each and every day God reveals to you what it means to be a true child of God as you are led by his Holy Spirit in the decisions you make.

My prayer is that you gain the ability to cry out to him "Abba, Father!" For as Galatians 4:6 says, "Because you are sons, God sent the Spirit of his Son into our hearts, the Spirit who calls out, "Abba, Father."

Right thinking according to the bible will lead to right believing and right living.

> *I pray that you grow in the fruits of God's spirit – love, joy, peace, patience, kindness, goodness, faithfulness, gentleness, and self control. For it is only in sharing this fruit with others that they will have the desire to taste and see that the Lord is good.*

This is what God desires – beauty that begins in the heart and outwardly expressed in glorifying him.

I pray this day that you commit to glorifying God in body and spirit this day and every day!

About the Author

"Just wanted to again thank you for sharing your unique and engaging presentation to help us take back our temples! You were truly a blessing and I know that many were enlightened by what you shared."

- *Danese Turner, Marietta GA*

When it comes to obesity issues, many speakers are like travel agents; they can tell you where to go, but have never been there. But Kimberly Taylor has the wisdom of a tour guide. Not only has she experienced the struggles of obesity firsthand, but she can help others get out of the diet pit—and stay out for life!

Kimberly Taylor has 15 years of health education and training experience through formal nursing practice (as an R.N. for many years) and research on the relationship between nutrition, physical activity, and chronic disease.

Kim's weight loss success story has been featured in *Prevention Magazine* (August 2008), *Charisma Magazine*, the *Atlanta Journal/Constitution*, and many other magazines and newspapers. She has also been interviewed for *The 700 Club* on CBN, *Essence Magazine*, and various radio programs.

Kim has a heart for others who struggle with weight and debt...once 240 pounds, a size 22, and in $19,000 worth of credit card debt, she can testify of God's goodness and healing power in these areas. Desperate to change her debt situation, she took a Crown Ministries (crown.org) course to learn how to manage money from a biblical perspective.

She used its principles to pay off her debt, and then used her new discipline to implement healthy eating and exercise habits. She was then able to achieve and maintain her ideal weight. This experience prompted her to establish **Take Back Your Temple**, whose title asks God to take control of your body and your life so He can use them for His purpose and agenda.

Kim's exhorts people of faith to become good stewards of all the resources God has given to them, including time, money, talents, and physical health. "I am passionate about empowering others to adopt healthy lifestyles so they can fulfill their God-given purpose," she says.

"My dream is for God's people to stand apart because we are healthy, prosperous and living the abundant life to which we are called. I want non-believers to look at us and want what we have: financial, spiritual, mental, and physical wholeness. Then when they ask us what we are doing differently, we can tell them about Jesus, the author and finisher of our faith.

2883644R00091

Printed in Great Britain
by Amazon.co.uk, Ltd.,
Marston Gate.